UNCLE TO**

WIDECOMBE I

First Published in 1996 by
Orchard Publications
2 Orchard Close, Chudleigh, Newton Abbot, Devon TQ13 0LR
Telephone: (01626) 852714

ISBN 1 898964 27 0

Photographs – Peter Hicks, page 28 Enid Shortridge.

Printed by
Hedgerow Print
Lapford, Devon EX17 6AE

AN INTRODUCTION TO UNCLE TOM COBLEY
Thomas Cobley – Uncle, Gent., and Mystery Maker

Events that took place in the 18th or 19th centuries, that led to the perpetuation of Thomas Cobley's name in rhyme and song, and continue to add considerably to the wealth of Widecombe, are cloaked in the type of merry mystery for which folk-lore and literature is renowned.

What is celebrated in song is generally recognised as something that couldn't have happened the way it is told but, like the Green Man of pagan lore, the song presents a face that is easily recognised and enjoyed by many, while it raises questions and hides some facts.

At least two contenders are put forward as being the Fair minded Tom Cobley. Sabine Baring-Gould directs attention towards a genial old bachelor, Thomas Cobley of Puddlecombe Park, Spreyton, who, being unable to read would reliably recite his will which was signed on January 20th 1787, and proved on March 14th 1794. Dying at the age of 99 years, this 'old' Uncle Thomas is said to be buried in Spreyton parish, but there is no sign of his grave. Likeable a contender though he may be, since it is claimed in Spreyton that Tom Cobley and his friends set out from there in September 1802 for Widecombe Fair, that traveller was obviously not the Thomas Cobley who had died eight years earlier.

A later generation of the Cobley lineage provides the second Uncle Tom Cobley contender, whose grave in Spreyton churchyard makes a starting point for but a continuing conundrum.

Thomas Cobley, Gent., late of Butsford in the parish of Colebrook departed this life on January 4th 1844 aged 82; and thereby continued the mystery.

W.G. Hoskins and S.H. Burton advise us that, "this Thomas Cobley is the *nephew* of the famous Uncle Tom Cobley, a substantial yeoman of Spreyton who died in the late 18th century at a great age after disinheriting his son Thomas for being too free with the girls, and who left his considerable estate to his nephew, who does not seem to even bothered to have erected a headstone to his benefactor".

Careful readers will have noted that while Baring-Gould refers to the 18th century Thomas Cobley of Puddlecombe Park as a genial bachelor, Hoskins and Burton tell us of his disreputable son; yet another Thomas Cobley and third possible contender for country fair fame. However, the Thomas Cobley of Colebrook parish was remembered locally as a highly respected, hard working wealthy man, a popular person and a sportsman who kept his own pack of hounds. His portrait shows him to have been a well built, weather beaten man with a humorous glint in his eye. Shown as a clean shaven man, might that glint in his eye have indicated that he was relishing the prospect of becoming the bewhiskered caricature character that history would turn him into? Thomas was certainly a busy man, so engrossed with work and daily activities that he found little time to devote to sitting for his portrait. So little in fact that the artist died, and completion of the picture was left to other talented hands.

The bare faced painting adds to a mystery which increases when we seek a solution from the song. If the song relates to the Widecombe Fair of 1802, then Thomas Cobley of Colebrook was at least 40 or 41 years old at that time and probably more than wealthy enough by that age to have owned horses; so why was one borrowed from Tom Pearce?

Could a horse even have been borrowed from Tom Pearce that year?

It is claimed that he who loaned the soon to be famous grey mare was one Thomas Pearse of Sticklepath, near Okehampton. Unfortunately, the relatively wealthy Pearses, who manufactured serge cloth, didn't move to Sticklepath to open their mill there until 1810.

But no matter. Definite events are related in song, without a reason for the ride being fully revealed. What mystery is perpetuated in rural rhyme while the date of the outing to Widecombe Fair and the true names and number of all those taking part is carefully concealed?

Did eight men, or more in total, good and true, continue on the way to Widecombe Fair, celebrating their arrival there, liberally, until none could stand to make the homeward march?

Thus, was an overloaded horse destined for fame for not carrying Tom Cobley home again, but into a place in history? The mystery remains while horse, and riders, long now lie content to let their song summon others to follow on; as content as any, who will follow Tom Cobley, God bless him, to Widecombe Fair.

VENTON – OUR NEW HOME

January 1948, I was just fifteen years old when for the very first time I stood at the top of Widecombe Hill and looked down on the village below and the surrounding countryside. Beyond Widecombe the ridge of Hamel Down stretched out for what seemed like miles, to my left Top Tor, Pil Tor and Blackslade Down and over my right shoulder Hound Tor with Hay Tor in the background. Of course I had heard of most of these places but never had the opportunity before of visiting them, and now they were going to be right on my doorstep, and in no time become as familiar to me as the fields we'd left behind in Torquay. Fifteen year olds don't use expressions like 'breathtaking' but thinking back to my feelings on that occasion, breathtaking it certainly was. I also remember thinking to myself, "This'll do me, we can have some good fun around these parts". The 'we' being me and my pony. My parents had just secured the tenancy of Higher Venton Farm, Widecombe, having several months previously been given notice to vacate our arable and dairy stock farm in Kingskerswell, on the outskirts of Torquay.

Higher Venton Farm was owned by Olive Katharine Parr, better known as Beatrice Chase the famous author. My parents were the successful applicants out of a total nearing two hundred. I think this was partly due to the generous character references provided by business and other associates my parents had made over the years. I remember the rent being £2 per week plus an extra £5 a year towards the upkeep of the thatched roof.

Although Venton Farm was also a dairy farm similar to the one we had left in Kingskerswell, the farming conditions on Dartmoor were, because of its very nature, completely different, and my father's advice to my three sisters and me was to "keep our mouths shut and our eyes wide open". I was now working full time as a farm hand for my father.

Whilst my family lived in the Venton farmhouse, Beatrice Chase lived in the adjoining Venton House. She proved to be a very difficult landlord and I remember my parents having several altercations with her. After allowing us to install a hot water heating system at our own expense she tried to terminate the tenancy on the grounds of the farm being mis-managed. In our opinion this was done in order to re-let the farm tenancy at a much higher rent because it now had the added advantage of running hot water. Following a farm inspection by the Agricultural Executive Committee which confirmed everything was being managed in a proper manner, she withdrew our notice.

On another occasion which we believed at the time to be an attempt to create publicity for her now fading career as a successful author, she informed the evening newspapers that Venton Farm had been destroyed by a fire caused through the neglect of her tenants. She'd seen smoke rising from the roof of one of the barns, when in fact it was me inside starting up a tractor. Not having seen the newspapers

4

1941, Foredown Farm, Kingskerswell, Torquay. I'm sat on the left in the top picture and on the right below. My father is in charge of the tractor and my pal is John Butcher. John was an evacuee from Surrey and stayed with us for four years during the Second World War. He fell in love with Devon and after the war he and his family spent many holidays with us. When his father died his mother purchased 'The Anchorage' (now named St. Anthonys), one of the cottages behind Venton, from my father, and retired to Devon. Sadly her retirement lasted only a few years and her ashes lay in Widecombe churchyard. The Anchorage was previously occupied by Bob Hitchcock, the last of Beatrice Chase's 'Blue Jackets' (male servants – all ex-naval men).

1951. Outside Higher Venton Farm. John, myself and Ben. John and I are still good friends and I am Godfather to his son. He still lives in Surrey and is a regular visitor to Venton.

ourselves we were somewhat surprised when attending Newton Abbot market the next morning folk kept asking us where we were going to live now our farm had burnt down. To cap it all a few days later the Chief Fire Officer for Torquay came over to inspect the damage. Another time she took a fall in the lane outside Venton and when my father and I helped her up she promptly accused us of assaulting her and even went so far as to call the police sergeant and a police constable from Ashburton to make an official complaint. When they heard our side of the story, and knowing her eccentricity, they took the matter no further. Her tetchiness was not reserved just for us, she directed it at pretty well everyone she came in contact with at some time or another. Not only did she own Venton farm but also the little row of three cottages which lie just behind the farm. Fred Miners and his wife used to rent one of them, St. Gabriels, and Beatrice was forever complaining to him about the dogs barking, his bonfire creating too much smoke and similar trivial matters. She'd write him notes and instead of walking a few yards and verbally complaining or put the note through his letterbox, she would pop it into the post box immediately outside Venton and the postman would have to deliver it.

We soon learnt to tolerate her mood swings and over the years I actually became quite close to her. She employed only male staff to care for her and upon dismissing her last 'blue jacket' asked me to do her daily chores. I was to be paid seven

6

shillings and sixpence a week, and if my memory serves me right I collected my first week's wage and that was all. I'd cook and clean for her, do her fires and even helped dress her. This went on for four years. She always slept with a loaded revolver under her pillow and I was the only person she mentioned it to. She became even more eccentric and during her final years ill-health swept over her. She died in July 1955. The day before her death she asked to see my parents and her final words to them were "Don't worry, Peter will be alright".

In her will she had bequeathed me Higher Venton Farm, albeit with a sizeable mortgage. This did not come as a total surprise, for on several occasions she told me I would be a beneficiary. In fact she seemed to take a perverse satisfaction in one day telling me I would benefit from her will and then a few days later informing me she had removed me from her will and was leaving all her worldly possessions to the 'cats and dogs home'. She did this at least six times in as many months towards the end of her life. She is buried in Widecombe Churchyard almost

opposite her mother's grave; an inscription on her headstone reads 'Pray for Olive Katharine Parr' and on the other side simply 'Beatrice Chase 1874 - 1955'.

My mother was elected treasurer of the Beatrice Chase Memorial Fund, set up to pay for the maintenance of her grave and headstone. Upon my mother's death the responsibility passed to me and the £150 still left in the fund I donated towards the cost of replacing the stained glass in the East window of the church. As church councillor and caretaker of the graveyard I still maintain the grave.

Beatrice's grave. The headstone reads 'Pray for Olive Katharine Parr' and on the other side 'Beatrice Chase 1874 - 1955'.

In her will she left Venton House and the little chapel which stands alongside to the Roman Catholic Bishop of Plymouth. Her three cottages which stand behind the farm she left to the R.S.P.C.A. As was the case with the farm all the properties carried mortgages. The new owners of the cottages and Venton House discharged the mortgages and put the properties up for sale on the open market. My father purchased the three cottages for £650 and at the subsequent auction of Venton House and the Chapel, bid up to £1,000, the property eventually being withdrawn unsold at £1,800. We presumed at the time it hadn't reached its reserve, yet three months later the auctioneers rang my father and asked if his offer of £1,000 still held good. Upon his confirmation to this effect they accepted his price and my family were now owners of Venton hamlet, together with Chittleford Farm, just a few hundred yards up the road, which my father had bought a few weeks earlier on the assumption that when Beatrice Chase died we may well have finished up homeless.

In 1957 my father offered me a partnership in our farming enterprise and the business became S. Hicks and Son. Venton and Chittleford comprised 150 acres and alongside our dairy herd we introduced some beef stock and a large number of Dartmoor ponies, which grazed out on the moor.

For several years I had been courting a local lass and when we married in Widecombe church during 1960 my parents moved into Venton House leaving my wife and I in the farmhouse. A few months later my father sold Chittleford Farm and retired, leaving me to farm Venton with obviously a much reduced dairy herd, although I still ran around eighty Dartmoor pony mares and three stallions. We always took the ponies to Chagford drift sales each autumn.

Around this time we started offering bed and breakfast accommodation which over the years has brought us many friends and visitors, a great number of whom have come to see where Beatrice Chase lived and wrote so much of her published work.

My father passed away in 1974 leaving Venton House to my mother, which upon her death a few years ago came to me. At this time I decided to retire from farming and let my grazing to other farmers, and to concentrate on our bed and breakfast business, along with the self catering accommodation we now offered from Venton House.

Although some of the village is older, much of Widecombe was built during the 16th century including Venton which actually dates to 1560. The porch over the farmhouse entrance was added in 1739 and the stone is inscribed to this effect.

At work in the churchyard

Chittleford 1956. My mother and father, and to my left Louise Deacon, another author and friend of Beatrice Chase.

Chittleford today.

WIDECOMBE FAIR

In spite of my father's advice to keep our mouths shut and our eyes wide open way back in 1948 to my sisters and me, or perhaps because of it, it wasn't long before I became involved with some of Widecombe's social events. Almost immediately I joined the Widecombe Fair committee and was soon made Agricultural Secretary, a position I held for seven years. The annual Widecombe Fair is always held on the second Tuesday of September. It is by far the most famous fair in Devonshire, if not the entire country. Records show a fair was held here in 1850 at which cattle and ponies were shown and sold, although it is very probable Widecombe held a sheep fair regularly for many years before the one recorded in 1850. Back in those days it was held on Widecombe Green alongside the church.

When I joined the committee, Widecombe Fair was quite a bit different to what it is nowadays. I remember the green playing host to a funfair which stayed on site for several days, and which on occasions went on till the next morning. The show field which held sheep shows, pony shows, tug-of-wars, pillow fights and lots, lots more attractions was then at Wooder Farm. The show field moved to its present site opposite the primary school during the 1950s.

Although the fair is now condensed into just the one day it has nevertheless grown considerably. The whole village is taken up with activity and the green is packed with small trading marquees selling everything from hot dogs and ice creams to T-shirts and trainers and even hoover parts. The show field houses the show ring where there are classes for Dartmoor and Shetland ponies, sheep and sheep dog displays, a parade of hounds, showjumping and a gymkhana for the children, to mention just a few of the attractions. Many local craft marquees and up-market trade stands along with the refreshment and bar facilities are also sited here.

The fair attracts thousands of visitors from far and wide and a one-way traffic system is introduced for the day to help congestion. The village is closed to traffic with cars and coaches directed to one of the many car parks brought into use. My advice to anyone coming along is to arrive early and stay for the day. There is always plenty to see and do and all the usual facilities are available.

According to a recent souvenir Widecombe fair programme the song used for the fair goes back 150 years or more and, although the words and tune varied according to whereabouts in the country it was performed, the Tom Pearse and Uncle Tom Cobley theme remained much the same. What is factual is that the folksong was first published by W. Davies of Kingsbridge in 1880 and re-published in 1889 by Sabine Baring-Gould. Not only was Baring-Gould a novelist and hymn writer, but he was also an expert on west country folklore and legends, and 'Widecombe Fair' featured in his collection of 1889, titled 'Songs and Ballads of the West'. He spent 43 years as squire and rector of Lewtrenchard, a village just off the A30 about 9 miles west of Okehampton. He became rector in 1881 and died in 1924. He is buried in the churchyard of the village he served so well, and legend has it that he conducted most of his writing standing up as though he was giving a sermon.

I have read that when Volunteers of the Devon Regiment were sent to the Boer War at the turn of the century, they used 'Widecombe Fair' as their marching song. How much truth lies within the actual wording of the song is open to conjecture, but it is generally agreed that the characters who figure in the chorus certainly did not all ride on the old grey mare – at least not all at the same time.

The verses of Widecombe Fair are reproduced later in the book.

Outside the Rugglestone Inn. This picture was taken several years ago – note the false beard. For the past four years I have sported home-grown whiskers.

Genuine whiskers – this visitor wants to know if Uncle Tom is ticklish.

UNCLE TOM COBLEY – MY ROLE

When I resigned my position as Agricultural Secretary to Widecombe Fair I became Sheep Steward, a position I filled until ten years ago when I undertook to play the part of Uncle Tom Cobley, and at the same time became an ordinary committee member. I succeeded local farmers Gordon Daw and Simon Northmore. Simon (Ned) had filled the role of Uncle Tom Cobley for twenty five years. Between us we are probably the most photographed riders in the county.

Preparing for the big day.

On the morning of Widecombe Fair day I put on my Uncle Tom garments and lead the fair procession through the village up to the show field; the rest of the day is spent riding around the village talking to the visitors, posing for photographs and signing autographs. For nine years the mare I rode was 'Glencoe' loaned to me for the day by the Shilstone Rocks Pony Stud at Chittleford. She generally had a good temperament for the job and was well behaved, but one year her owner decided to fit her with blinkers for the day. She had not worn them before and I was not too keen on the suggestion but the owner had the last word and the blinkers were duly fitted. Everything was going along quite well until a dog barked right behind us as we were walking through the show field. A startled Glencoe leapt up in the air and promptly jumped over the bonnet of a red Ford Escort, and as she did so I heard a loud 'clonk' of horseshoe on metal. As I struggled to bring her under control I heard a voice nearby call out "Cor, bugger, he can ride a bit too".

I returned later during the afternoon to inspect the damage and found a lovely hoof print right in the centre of the Escort's bonnet – that was one Widecombe visitor who took home at least one more Widecombe Fair souvenir than intended.

In 1995 I rode my own mare 'Sunset Grey Lady', although we call her by her stable name of 'Tidy'. She is a fifteen year old Arab cross bred and should carry me around the Fair for a good few years to come.

There was a time when I could spring up into the saddle, but now 'Old Uncle Tom' has to use a mounting block or a convenient set of steps.

AROUND WIDECOMBE

Although I have lived in Widecombe for nearly fifty years, married a local lass and raised our own family here in the village, I'll be the first to admit there are other locals far better qualified than me to take the reader on an exploration of Widecombe. However, over the years I have come to love this village and feel more than able to take the visitor on a ramble through our beautiful lanes, pointing out the places of interest and in particular those places which over the years have meant so much to me.

The village is well served with car parking facilities, the most convenient one being found adjoining the coach park opposite the Green and, for the purpose of this book, I will consider this to be the starting point of a Widecombe exploration. An information board is sited next to the toilets giving visitors a brief description of the village.

The much photographed granite cross sitting proudly on the Green between the road and church wall bears a plaque stating it was given to the parish by Francis Hamlyn Esquire from Dunstone Court in 1948. It also displays the old grey mare with the seven characters mounted and one with a lead rope. Widecombe Green, or Butte Park by its proper name, offers visitors a resting place and picnic spot. Its name is derived from an Act of Parliament passed in 1466 which directed 'every Englishman should have a bow of his own height of yew, ash, wychhazel or amburn, and that butts should be made in every township on which the inhabitants were to shoot every feast day under the penalty of a halfpenny when they should omit that exercise'. I have a very old book on Widecombe in which the Green is quoted as being an old 'Archery practice ground'.

St. Pancras Church is often referred to as the 'Cathedral of the Moor' although I have also heard it called the 'Dartmoor Cathedral'. The church was built in the 14th century although the tower is thought to have been added during the early 16th century. The four pinnacled tower stands 135 feet high and its building was financed by the Dartmoor tin miners. High in the barrel roof above the communion rails one of the bosses displays the three rabbits, a symbol closely associated with that of the tinners. The church welcomes visitors and offers its own little guide book and roof bosses leaflet which offer far more information than I have room to detail in this book.

Being a Church councillor I obviously have great affection for my church. In September 1960 my wife and I were married here, both our daughters were christened here and although my parents are not buried in Widecombe, services for them were held here before they left the village. I have always felt great peace and serenity whenever entering the church and I know my family and friends also find it of great comfort.

Above: My mother and father with my elder sister Diana and my two daughters Margaret (the taller) and Helen.

Left: My mother and father, Bet and I – Margaret's christening.

However, it wasn't so peaceful on October 21st 1638, for it was on this day a tremendous thunderstorm passed over Dartmoor. As the storm neared Widecombe a Sunday afternoon service was being conducted by the minister of the parish, George Lyde. A great darkness prevailed, preventing the congregation from reading their books, accompanied by far reaching forks of lightning and the inevitable thunder. The lightning struck the tower causing one of the pinnacles to crash down on the congregation below, and a fireball tore through the church. Four parishioners were killed instantly and between fifty and sixty suffered burns and other injuries. George Lyde escaped injury but his wife suffered serious burns.

As the storm abated one of the locals, Ralph Rouse, stood up and said "Neighbours, in the name of God, shall we venture out of the church?" George Lyde replied, "It is best to make an end of prayers, for it were better to die here than in another place". But the remaining congregation were not convinced and looking around at the damage and injuries sustained turned and ran out of the church. Four wallboards inside the church tell the story of the storm.

A publication I have which was written in 1874 gives mention of the thunderstorm in great detail and apparently other areas in the west country were also greatly affected. Of course it wasn't long before the storm was seized upon and made out to be the work of the Devil. It soon became legend and now many books on Dartmoor recall the day 'the Devil called at Widecombe'. Apparently on the fateful day a stranger had stopped at the Tavistock Inn at Poundsgate and as he drank his ale his throat sizzled causing the innkeeper to observe "'Twas the Devil a visiting". He leapt upon his horse and rode off towards Widecombe leaving payment for his ale on the bar top. As soon as he was out of sight the coins turned to dried leaves. Upon reaching the church the Devil tied his horse to one of the spires and then reached down into the church and seized on one Jan Reynolds, who had reneged on an agreement made several years previously with Satan. As he loosed his horse he wrenched one of the pinnacles from its position and threw it down into the congregation. The pair then galloped off over Dartmoor and poor Jan was never seen again, but Widecombe was left to mourn the Devil's revenge.

One year whilst I was acting the role of Uncle Tom Cobley an elderly visitor said to me, "Your church has got four spires, and yet I've read that one was thrown down by the Devil". I replied, "That's right my dear, and when the Devil had disappeared God raised his hand and the spire jumped right back up again".

The granite cross which is found outside near the south porch is thought to be the original village cross, which once stood in the square west of the church where the yew tree now grows. It is possible the cross dates back before the church itself and was the meeting place for services before the church was built.

The Church House was built nearly 500 years ago and is now owned by The National Trust. Its original purpose was to serve as a resting place for chuchgoers who may have walked many a mile to their place of worship. Most country villages provided a similar premise and many of them were later converted into pubs, and that is why there are so many Church House Inns around. Over the years the Church House has served many roles; ale house, a poor house, at one time it was made into several almshouses, and earlier this century it was used as the village school. Nowadays part of it is used as the village hall, and Sexton's Cottage, which is incorporated into the building, is a National trust retail outlet. Standing outside the Church House is a 15 inch Naval shell which was presented to Widecombe in 1920 by the National War Savers Committee in recognition of the villagers' effort during the First World War in gathering sphagnum moss from the moor which was used in the treatment of wounds.

Opposite the Church House stands Glebe House, again dating back to the early 16th century, as does so much of the building in Widecombe. The dictionary's definition of Glebe is 'land granted to a clergyman as part of his benefice' and Glebe House was built on land formerly owned by the vicar. It is now a fascinating shop displaying all things Widecombe including Uncle Tom Cobley's chair, although this is one Uncle Tom Cobley who personally has never sat in it. The shop is owned by Percy Middleweek who has an interest in one or two other retail outlets in the village. Percy has traded here for more years than I can remember.

Forming the fourth side of the village square are The Old Inn and the Old Smithy. The Inn dates back further than its previously mentioned neighbours – to the 14th century in fact. It was used as a coaching house and in all probability as a court house, both a magistrates court and a stannary court. A stannary is an area where tin is mined and for several hundreds of years tin was extracted in varying quantities from much of Dartmoor. Ashburton was one of the four stannary towns – the others being Tavistock, Plympton and Chagford – and these served as collection and distribution centres for the smelted metal, and for the collection of coinage duty. The tinners were governed by many of their own laws and cases in district courts were decided by a jury made up of tinners. With Ashburton being so close to Widecombe it is more than likely some of those cases may well have been conducted in The Old Inn.

The Inn is very popular and I must confess it is one of my 'locals'. The food, drink and service are superb and even during the depths of winter the car park at the rear is full to capacity during weekend lunchtimes. It is also haunted, but don't let this put you off its fayre, for although I've seen a few 'spirits' in the bar I've never seen the ghost.

The Old Smithy was a blacksmith's shop until the 1950s. I can recall taking our horses there for shoeing when first coming to Widecombe. Upon its closure it became a museum and now it is a pottery shop. A sign above the shop says 'The Old Forge. Established 200 years', problem is when was the sign erected? The building itself is probably as old as the inn next door and the blacksmith's trade must go back certainly to the 16th century.

Just down from the Old Smithy is the post office and immediately opposite on the grass verge are two granite stones. These are mounting blocks for horse riders and as the large house behind is the old vicarage, it is reasonable to assume they would have been used by parishioners on leaving, having had an audience with the vicar. The old vicarage is now privately owned.

A few yards on from the post office visitors will find the old Saxon Well. The well used to be the main water supply for the village and locals will tell you it has never run dry. I find it rather surprising the well was regarded as the village's main water supply; this can only be because of its convenient position, as the sparkling clear waters of the East Webburn River flow within a few hundred yards of this spot. Incidentally, the well was in use until the 1940s but drinking from it now is not recommended.

I suggest leaving the village by walking back to the square and taking the

narrow lane leading downhill between the churchyard and Glebe House. After about 200 yards the road passes over the East Webburn River via Venton Bridge. The river rises a few miles away on Hamel Down and from Widecombe flows under Cockingford Bridge, about a mile downstream, and meets up with the West Webburn before flowing into the River Dart just below Buckland in the Moor. To me the Webburn Valley is one of the most beautiful parts of Dartmoor.

The large bungalow on the right hand side immediately after crossing Venton Bridge is our new Rectory. A little way further on is the second (or first, depending on which way I'm walking) of my 'locals', the Rugglestone Inn. The inn is named after the Rugglestone rock which lies a few hundred yards to the west and can only be reached via Widecombe Hill. The Rugglestone rock is said to weigh over 100 tons and rests upon a smaller stone; legend says that one would rock upon the other upon the insertion of the church key. I have never seen any movement and doubt the probability of it ever having done so. The Rugglestone is a boundary mark between the two manors of Dunstone and Widecombe and also forms the north boundary of Venton Farm.

The Rugglestone Inn is very small by comparison with the Old Inn and consists of just two rooms – one dispensing the drinks and the other dispensing the food. But don't let this put you off, whatever it might lack in size it more than makes up for in the quality of both its ale and its food. It is listed in the 1995 Egon Ronay guide. The pub offers a large car park a few yards further on and a large beer garden with tables is open during the seasonal months.

From the Rugglestone the little road takes you past Venton and on to Chittleford, where you will find the Shilstone Rocks Pony Stud. This is the farm my father owned before Beatrice Chase died, and sold to the present owner in the early 1960s. The stud was founded in 1962 and breed pure-bred Dartmoor ponies, unlike the majority found on the open moor which are cross-bred.

Chittleford Farm is one of the oldest buildings to be found around Widecombe. Records go back to the early 13th century, but it is quite probably several hundreds of years older than this. Its main feature is the granite archway and passage.

My nearest local – the Rugglestone Inn.

The lane from Venton leads to the Rugglestone Inn. The bungalow to the left is our new Rectory and Widecombe Church can just be made out in the background.

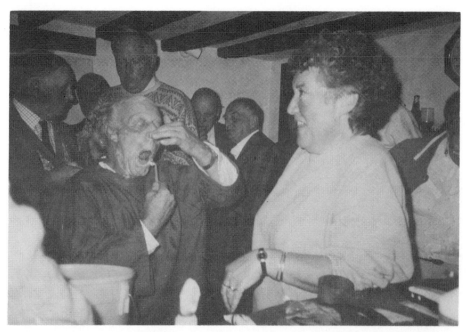

The beard comes off after Widecombe Fair. A sponsored shave which has raised more than £1,200 over the last three years.

A clean shaven 'Uncle Tom'.

The high moor behind Chittleford is Blackslade Down and a few hundred yards up the road is found the privately owned Blackslade House. As a boy I can remember having lunch here whilst beating the manor bounds.

A mile and a half or so from Widecombe and this little road meets up with

The lane to Venton.

another on what is now Pudsham Down. By turning right here a walk down hill of about half a mile brings us to Cockingford Bridge, carrying the road over the East Webburn once again. Five minutes up from the bridge and the walker comes to another junction where by turning right a walk of about a mile leads to the centre of Widecombe, but don't be in too great a hurry when passing through the hamlet of Dunstone or you will miss Dunstone Court. Just a few yards down a little lane leading off to the right, which incidentally leads to Chittleford and the pony stud, is Dunstone Court.

Dunstone Court was owned until a few years ago by the Hamlyn Family who date back many generations to the 13th century. The reader will recall it was Francis Hamlyn who gave the granite cross standing on the green alongside the church wall to the parish of Widecombe in 1948.

The cross standing on the little green nearby was restored to Dunstone in 1980

Dunstone Cross.

by Mary Hamlyn after spending over 100 years in the garden of the old vicarage. It was taken from Dunstone in 1845 by Rev. James Holman Mason for safe keeping, having been knocked over and vandalised. Near here also lies a large granite rock and it was here that the annual payments were made by the farmers and the tenants for the right to run their stock, cut peat and extract gravel from the moor. Although we are still allowed to graze our stock the latter privileges have now been withdrawn.

From Dunstone the road soon leads into the village passing the main showground of Widecombe Fair on the right and the primary school on the left. Just past the school stands a row of three old cottages, the middle one of which used to be the village bakery.

The middle cottage used to be the village bakery.

From the centre of the village one road runs north towards Moretonhampstead, although turnings on the right and left on the way will take you to North Bovey and Chagford also. The car park to the rear of the popular Old Inn is passed after a few yards and a little further on a track leads off to the left, sign-posted Hamel Down (Hameldon). This track takes the walker high onto the crest of Hamel Down and an hour's walk along its ridge eventually leads to the Bronze Age village of Grimspound, having passed Hamel Down Beacon, three barrows and Hameldown Tor on the way. On a fine weather day the views from the ridge are magnificent, Princetown and beyond one way, Haytor and the distant coastline the other, Exmoor many miles ahead and the South Hams many miles behind. The barrows or burrows are ancient graves and excavations have revealed burnt human bones. Whilst extolling its beauty in good weather, beware Hamel Down in bad – the mist and fog can descend in minutes and the wind blows so strong sometimes it feels likely to carry you off, and of course when the snow falls, whilst Widecombe village can remain snow free, the ridge can be inches deep.

One of the 24 hut circles in Grimspound, a Middle Bronze Age settlement about 3,000 years old. Grimspound is one of the best known prehistoric structures on the moor, and easily visited by road. It lies just off the Widecombe to Moretonhampstead road, about 4 miles from Widecombe. There is a small lay-by for parking, and from there you can see the old tin workings in the valley below. Grimspound is not clearly visible from the road, but there is a small track opposite the lay-by on the other side of the road that clearly marks the way.

This track follows the course of the Grims Lake, a small stream that runs through part of the walled enclosure. Approaching from this angle does tend to mislead people, as they come across a breach in the compound wall that looks like the main entrance. It is, in fact, a later opening, fashioned when the road from Manaton to Headland Warren was made, which runs right through Grimspound. My advice to visitors is to walk up the path from the road and bear left, climbing the slope to the top of Hookney (Hookner) Tor. From there you will have a wonderful view of Grimspound and the original main entrance on the far side of the enclosure.

Walkers can find it by following the Two Moors Way along the ridge of Hamel Down. The Rev. Sabine Baring-Gould, who I have mentioned several times before, carried out an exploration dig at Grimspound along with members of the Dartmoor Exploration Committee between 1894/96, and it is as a result of this dig along with previous surveys conducted in 1829 and 1855, that we know so much about this site.

As a youngster I spent many happy hours along here on my pony.

The road north passes Wooder Manor, now offering holiday accommodation; Bagpark and Natsworthy before leaving Widecombe far behind. Bagpark Manor farm is privately owned and houses a deer farm. The little river running alongside the road for a good way is once again the East Webburn, which rises near Natsworthy. Between Lower and Middle Natsworthy a track, which soon becomes a small path between the fields, leads off to the right and a walk of twenty minutes along this path brings you to Jay's grave, the supposed resting place of a young suicide girl named Kitty Jay, who early last century hanged herself having been taken advantage of by a local young squire. The grave is frequently decorated with fresh flowers, a gesture Beatrice Chase often conducted.

However, before Natsworthy, a few hundred yards past the entrance to Bagpark and immediately before a cattle grid, a stoney track leads off to the right which soon levels out and passes beneath Honeybag Tor, Chinkwell Tor and Bell Tor before returning to Widecombe village, via Bonehill.

As a circular walk from the village this walk takes about 1½ hours.

Having explored some of the attractions north of the village the aforementioned Bonehill can also be found by leaving Widecombe on the road south – namely Widecombe Hill – the way 'in' for most of our visitors. After walking down hill past the cafe a minor road leads off to the left, and after taking this route soon crosses over the East Webburn River. A little further on the walker reaches Bonehill House and the hamlet of Bonehill Farms which lie beneath Bonehill Rocks. Most of Bonehill or 'Bunhill' as it is recorded in the old Widecombe registers, dates back to the early 16th century, but it is very probable farming was carried out here several hundreds of years before this and in its very primitive way back to the Bronze Age, 2,000 - 3,000 years ago. The buildings are predominantly granite and even from the road enough can be seen to appreciate the rugged architecture of nearly five hundred years ago. Lower Bonehill is a fine example of a fine old medieval longhouse, which has recently been restored.. Opposite is found Bonehill Farm, another original longhouse, with its date of restoration inscribed on the porch. I've often heard Bonehill Rocks called Bunny Tor – presumably taken from the old register name of 'Bunhill', although it could be because of the large population of 'four legged furry things about these parts'. Where Bonehill Lane greets the open moor it passes between two granite pillars either side of the road and although my family were living in Kingskerswell at the time and I was just a boy, I can recall a tremendous thunderstorm one night in 1938 which washed the road away to such a depth at this point that locals reckoned you could have driven a horse and cart under the gate which used to span the two pillars.

Bonehill House itself is not quite so old as the rest of the hamlet and until 1900 was just a small cottage. It was purchased by a London businessman who built onto the cottage and added a groom's cottage and stables in the grounds, naming it Bonehill Villa. It has changed ownership since and the groom's cottage is now a crafts studio.

Out on the moor 'pony gathering' for the Autumn drift sales at Chagford.

BEATRICE CHASE

Most books on Dartmoor and certainly those written about Widecombe will in some part mention Beatrice Chase, real name Katharine Olive Parr, famous author. Because of her influence on my life this book shall not be the exception. Certainly she was a very complex woman and often very difficult to deal with. She considered herself to be an authority on Dartmoor which I always took with a pinch of salt. How can anybody be an authority on such a place as this with its vastness, its remoteness and its changing moods. She loved Dartmoor dearly, of that there is no dispute, and it is for this mutual feeling we shared and often spoke that I will remember her with affection.

Olive Katharine Parr, a descendant of William Parr, brother of Katherine, wife of Henry VIII, was born in Harrow, Middlesex, in 1874. During her late twenties she developed tuberculosis, probably as a result of working alongside her mother in the London workhouses, where the disease was prevalent. Doctors advised her to take a holiday in the west country where the air was still pure, and so they came to Dartmoor, to Widecombe, and quite simply they stayed.

Venton at this time was a Devon longhouse which Beatrice and her mother occupied for holiday purposes. When they decided not to return to London they realised larger accommodation was needed if they were to reside permanently on Dartmoor, and reluctantly they put Venton up for sale. Then one day whilst in conversation with local builder and mason, William Warren, she asked him if it would be possible to extend the existing cottage. As a result, several months later, her tiny moorland chapel was opened with the main extension, 'Venton House' being completed within another four weeks, September 1908. Beatrice was overjoyed, for she had never wanted to leave Venton, and when William Warren died nearly forty years later, she said, 'I am sure, for the joy given to countless people from all over the world who have visited Venton and its chapel, William has a special reward and joy in his heavenly home'.

Under her pen name, Beatrice soon started writing her short stories and other works of fiction and non fiction, a lot of it based on the people and places of Dartmoor. Through her books the British public were drawn to Dartmoor, to seek out the attractions for themselves, and of course to visit Venton – to see the Darmoor window where she sat whilst writing most of her work. She even opened a little book shop at Venton selling her various publications. She became famous and probably her best books, and certainly her best sellers were 'Through a Dartmoor Window' and 'The Heart of the Moor', written about seventy years ago.

Several of her books can still be purchased in local second hand bookshops, and although her popularity certainly waned towards the end of her life, the interest in her now seems as strong as ever, and good condition second hand copies command a fair price. Positively thousands of her books were destroyed when, during a German bombing raid on London on 29th December 1940, a direct hit wiped out her publisher's warehouse.

She never told me about any romantic connection she had but I understand she lost her fiance in the First World War. Upon his death she turned to her Roman Catholic faith for comfort and her chapel. Here she kept a Roll of Honour with the names of husbands and sweethearts fighting in the trenches, sent to her by their wives and girlfriends. Every day she would pray for them, and she even had sent to her a Military Cross and DSO from a soldier who had returned safely after seeing action in the Battle of Vimy Ridge, and was convinced her prayers for his well-being were answered.

When she died her death went virtually unnoticed and to my knowledge only one daily newspaper reported her passing. Apart from my family only a few people attended her funeral – if she had passed away twenty years earlier Widecombe wouldn't have been able to accommodate the mourners. But as I

have said previously, nowadays there still seems to be great interest in Beatrice Chase and her books, and every summer season we get holiday-makers staying with us so as they return home saying they have stayed where Beatrice Chase lived. And still we get photographers and artists taking photos of and painting the Dartmoor window and Venton. Perhaps like Beatrice I should open a bookshop.

The Chapel, Venton. Visitors have often felt a 'presence' in here, and certainly my family has witnessed some strange happenings.

Beatrice Chase

Venton House extension, completed September, 1908.

Higher Venton Farm.

*Uncle Tom Cobley outside Higher
Venton Farm, which offers
visitors Bed and Breakfast
accommodation along with self
catering in Venton House.*

*Uncle Tom and Mrs Uncle Tom
(Bet).*

THE BALLAD OF WIDECOMBE FAIR

Tom Pearse, Tom Pearse, lend I the Grey Mare
All along, down along, out along Lee,
Vur us wants vur to go over to Widdicombe Fair,

*Wi' Bill Brewer, Jan Stewer, Peter Gurney, Peter Davy, Dan'l Whiddon,
    Harry Hawk,*
Old Uncle Tom Cobleigh and all, Old Uncle Tom Cobleigh and all.

An' when shall I see again th' Grey Mare?
All along, down along, out along Lee,
By Vriday noon or Satuday soon.

But Vriday came and Saturday soon,
All along, down along, out along Lee,
An' Tom Pearse's auld Mare 'er hath not trotted home.

So Tom Pearse 'e went up to the top of the 'ill,
All along, down along, out along Lee,
An' 'e zeed 'is auld Mare down amakin' 'er will.

Now Tom Pearse's auld Mare 'er tuke sick an' 'er died,
All along, down along, out along Lee,
An' Tom Pearse 'e sat down on a stone an' he cried.

Now this isn't the end o' this shockin' affair
All along, down along, out along Lee,
Nor, though they be dead, o' th' 'orrid career.

When the wind whistles cold on the moor of a night,
All along, down along, out along Lee,
Tom Pearse's auld Mare doth appear ghostly white.

An' all the night long be heard skirlin' an' groans,
All along, down along, out along Lee,
From Tom Pearse's auld Mare an' 'er rattlin' bones.

Other Dartmoor titles available from Orchard Publications:
Around Princetown's Quarries by John Hallet – P/back £5.95
The Ancient Dwellings of Grimspound & Hound Tor by Lesley Chapman
                                                    – P/back £2.95
The Dartmoor Stannaries by Paul Hambling – P/back £3.95
The Mysterious Lady of the Moor by Judy Chard – P/back £3.99
Mining and Quarrying in the Teign Valley by Stafford Clark – P/back £4.50
The Dartmoor Puzzler No. 1 (a quiz book for all) – P/back £1.20
The Dartmoor Puzzler No. 2 (a quiz book for all) – P/back £1.30

For a full title list write to:
Orchard Publications, 2 Orchard Close, Chudleigh, Newton Abbot,
Devon TQ13 0LR, enclosing S.A.E.